This book is dedicated to the Spirit of Adventure and its best friends: Risk and Uncertain Outcome.

An adventurous life is worth living.

My greatest thanks go to Jana Ley, my wife, who has supported my adventurous life for over 45 years. And thank you to the many friends, family, and colleagues who have supported this project with time, energy, and beer: Jim Davidson, Andy Nelson, Sam Ley, Lucas Mouttet, Mike Soucy, Owen Richard, Davis Rice, Larry Chapman, and others too numerous to remember. And finally, thank you to Andy Sovick and the Beacon Guidebooks team for their support and inspiration.

About the Author: Rodney Ley

Rodney Ley began skiing in 1964 on wooden skis with cable bindings and lace-up leather boots. Most of his friends think he should be a better skier by now! Rodney first skied on Cameron Pass in 1972 and it remains his favorite spot to ski. In 1985, Rodney founded the Never Summer Nordic Yurt System in the Colorado State Forest, one of the first backcountry yurt systems in the U.S. He served as the Cameron Pass avalanche observer for the Colorado Avalanche Information Center from 1986 to 1991. In 1990, Rodney began a 30-year career as director of the Outdoor Program at Colorado State University. His proudest moments are summiting 22 peaks above 15,000' with CSU students on three continents.

From the publisher:

Without our team of incredible specialists, these books and maps would not be possible. Graphic design by Keitha Kostyk, aerial images by Alex Ne... (Summit Aerial Media), cartography by ... (Singletrack Maps), and editing by Emm...

Get the book and map on your...

Downloadable for offline use, each o... is available in digital form. With the ... button, you get access to GPS naviga... our aerial photos, route descriptions... and more. Shop for your digital guid... here on the Beacon Guidebooks web...

3

BACKCOUNTRY RESCUE AND EDUCATION SINCE 1990.

THANK YOU TO OUR PARTNERS

Larimer County Sheriff's Emergency Services
Larimer County Search and Rescue
Arapaho-Roosevelt National Forest
Jackson County Sheriff's Office and Search and Rescue
Colorado Parks and Wildlife- State Forest State Park
Rocky Mountain National Park

IN THE CASE OF AN EMERGENCY CALL 911
Try this first. If it works then follow their instructions.

IF 911 DOESN'T WORK:
1. Use the SOS feature of a personal locator device such as InReach or Spot.
2. Flag down and ask for assistance from fellow skiers or drivers.
3. Make your way west to the Moose Visitor Center or east to the Spencer Heights call box.

After you make contact, it may take several hours for help to arrive.
Be prepared to spend the night out on any backcountry trip.

MORE INFO & DONATE

DIAMOND PEAKS SKI PATROL IS A NON-PROFIT MEMBER OF THE ROCKY MOUNTAIN DIVISION IN THE NATIONAL SKI PATROL SYSTEM.

VOLUNTEER POWERED | DONATION FUNDED | ACCEPTING NEW RECRUITS

BACKCOUNTRY SKIING ETHICS + BEST PRACTICES

The growing popularity of backcountry skiing in Colorado has exceeded all prior expectations. Skills and behaviors that were once assumed to take years to develop are now expected immediately of new-to-the-sport backcountry skiers and riders. To better understand these community expectations please review these ethics and best practices for the safety and enjoyment of all users.

LEAVE NO TRACE

Leave No Trace Seven Principles

1. Plan Ahead and Prepare
2. Travel and Camp on Durable Surfaces
3. Dispose of Waste Properly
4. Leave What You Find
5. Minimize Campfire Impacts
6. Respect Wildlife
7. Be Considerate of Other Visitors

© Leave No Trace: www.LNT.org

Setting and Using Skintracks

This atlas includes commonly used approaches for each sector, but conditions and circumstances may dictate other options. Knowing good etiquette for setting community-minded skintracks minimizes user conflict.

✔ Set skintracks with an eye to safety and the lowest possible risk
✔ Avoid unnecessarily steep terrain or multiple switchbacks
✔ Keep skintracks off the slopes being skied or ridden down
✔ Never walk or snowshoe on a ski skintrack
✔ Step aside to allow faster skiers to pass you

Preparing for a Backcountry Ski Trip

Effective planning for a backcountry skiing day involves aspects of safety, comfort, and communication. Allow every member of your party to have an equal part in determining routes, safety, and risk tolerance.

✔ Read the daily weather and avalanche report before arriving at the trailhead
✔ Compare the avalanche report to the terrain you plan to ski or ride
✔ Confirm your party has the appropriate safety gear (beacon, probe, shovel) and the knowledge to properly use it
✔ Consider the use of advanced safety gear: avalanche airbag, radios, and GPS devices
✔ Check that your party has appropriate over-the-snow travel gear for the intended terrain
✔ Ensure that adequate clothing, accessories, food, and water is carried by each party member

Dogs and Backcountry Skiing

Few issues can provoke more strong opinions than taking dogs on backcountry ski trips. Regardless of your decision whether or not to bring a dog, consider the ramifications to all users.

✔ Do not put an avalanche beacon on your dog that has the same radio frequency as human-worn beacons
✔ Dogs should always be under full leash or voice control to avoid entering avalanche terrain and to prevent user conflict
✔ Provide full pet first aid, winter injury care, food, and water for your dog
✔ Be prepared with the knowledge and equipment to evacuate your dog if necessary

TABLE OF CONTENTS

USEFUL TOOLS IN THIS GUIDE

Our graphics are designed to give you a quick reference to some of the key elements in your decision-making process.

General Aspect
The general direction all runs in a particular zone will face.

ATES Ratings
We label and color all zones and descents according to their ATES ratings. *See page 9* to learn more about ATES.

Max Slope Angle / Descent Elevation Loss

Ascent Line

Descent Line

Ascend / Descend

Yurt or Hut

Avalanche Terrain Information

Parking / Trailhead / Skintrack Start

Access / Ascent / Skintrack Information

Exit Information

Parking Lot / Area

Snowmobile Access

EVERY LOCATION IN THIS ATLAS IS PRIME AVALANCHE TERRAIN.

Every location in this book is prime avalanche terrain. The terrain of the Cameron Pass backcountry is steep with varying levels of exposure to avalanche activity. Beacon Guidebooks uses the ATES rating system to help readers understand that variation and choose tours that match the risk described in the CAIC daily avalanche forecast.

Avalanche safety is extremely important for anyone recreating in the mountains of Colorado.

GET THE FORECAST

KNOW THE DIAMOND PEAKS SKI PATROL COMMUNICATIONS

KNOW THE CDOT ROAD CONDITIONS

NORTH AMERICAN AVALANCHE DANGER SCALE

EXTREME
Avoid all avalanche terrain.

HIGH
Very dangerous avalanche conditions. Travel in avalanche terrain not recommended.

CONSIDERABLE
Dangerous avalanche conditions. Careful snowpack evaluation, cautious route-finding and conservative decision making are essential.

MODERATE
Heightened avalanche conditions on specific terrain features. Evaluate snow and terrain carefully; identify features of concern.

LOW
Generally safe avalanche conditions. Watch for unstable snow on isolated terrain features.

NO RATING
Watch for signs of unstable snow such as recent avalanches, cracking in the snow and audible collapsing. Avoid traveling on or under similar slopes.

ALL BEACON GUIDEBOOKS MAPS AND ATLASES USE THE ATES SYSTEM.

ATES (Avalanche Terrain Exposure Scale) is a planning tool designed and used extensively in Canada. It helps identify appropriate terrain for the avalanche hazard of the day, but it does not predict the stability of a given slope. *Source: Government of Canada. Parks Canada. pc.gc.ca/en.*

Our authors characterize and classify the terrain of each sector of their backcountry zone. Once classified, we fit them into one of three categories: 1-Simple, 2-Challenging, or 3-Complex. The definitions are below. These green, blue, and black, colors should not be confused with the difficulty of a run (like we are used to seeing in a ski resort). **Green** means: Simple avalanche terrain. **Blue** means: Challenging avalanche terrain. **Black** means: Complex avalanche terrain.

 **SIMPLE ZONES**

Exposure to low angle or primarily forested terrain. Some forest openings may involve the runout zones of infrequent avalanches and terrain traps may exist. Many options to reduce or eliminate exposure.

SIMPLE ROUTES

offer options to reduce your exposure to avalanche terrain in Challenging zones.

 CHALLENGING ZONES

Exposure to well defined avalanche paths, starting zones, terrain traps or overhead hazard. Options exist to reduce or eliminate exposure with careful routefinding.

CHALLENGING ROUTES

offer options to reduce your exposure to avalanche terrain in **Complex** zones.

 COMPLEX ZONES

Exposure to multiple overlapping avalanche paths or large expanses of steep, open terrain. Sustained exposure to overhead hazard. Many avalanche starting zones and terrain traps with minimal options to reduce exposure.

CHALLENGING ROUTES

increase your exposure to higher consequence avalanche terrain.

Study the terrain in this book and on our topo map. Understand how it relates to the ATES scale, and what kind of objective hazards each tour might be exposed to.

Get the avalanche forecast. Then, using the Avaluator, connect the avalanche danger rating with the terrain rating of the area you plan on visiting to provide a recommendation on what level of caution should be taken given the forecasted avalanche conditions. You can then decide whether or not to proceed or go somewhere else.

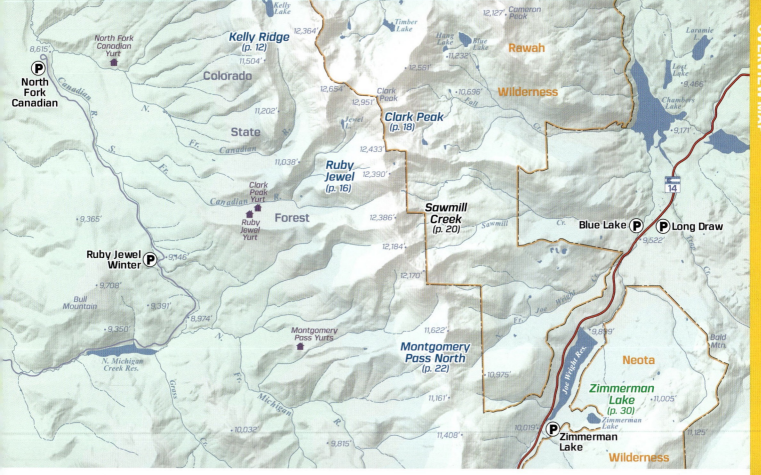

North Fork Canadian Yurt

8,615'
Ⓟ North Fork Canadian

Kelly Lake

Kelly Ridge (p. 12)
11,504'

Colorado

12,364'

Timber Lake

12,127' Cameron Peak

Rawah

Hang Lake

Blue Lake

• 11,232

Laramie L.

Lost Lake
• 9,466'

Wilderness

Chambers Lake

12,561'

Canadian R.

11,202'

State

12,654'

12,951'

Clark Peak

• 10,696'

• 9,171'

N.

Fr.

S.

11,038'

Clark Peak (p. 18)

Jewel L.

12,433'

Ruby Jewel (p. 16)

12,390'

14

• 9,365'

Clark Peak Yurt

Canadian

R.

Forest

12,386'

Sawmill Creek (p. 20)

Sawmill

Cr.

Blue Lake Ⓟ Ⓟ Long Draw

9,522'

Ruby Jewel Yurt

Ruby Jewel Winter Ⓟ

• 9,146'

12,184'

• 9,708'

Bull Mountain

• 9,391'

12,170'

• 9,350'

• 8,974'

N.

Montgomery Pass Yurts

11,622'

• 9,899'

Bald Mtn.

N. Michigan Creek Res.

Fr.

Montgomery Pass North (p. 22)

Joe Wright

Neota

Fr.

• 10,975'

Grass

Michigan

11,161'

Joe Wright Res.

Zimmerman Lake (p. 30)

• 11,005'

• 10,032'

R.

Cr.

• 9,815'

11,408'

10,019'

Ⓟ Zimmerman Lake

Zimmerman Lake

11,125'

Wilderness

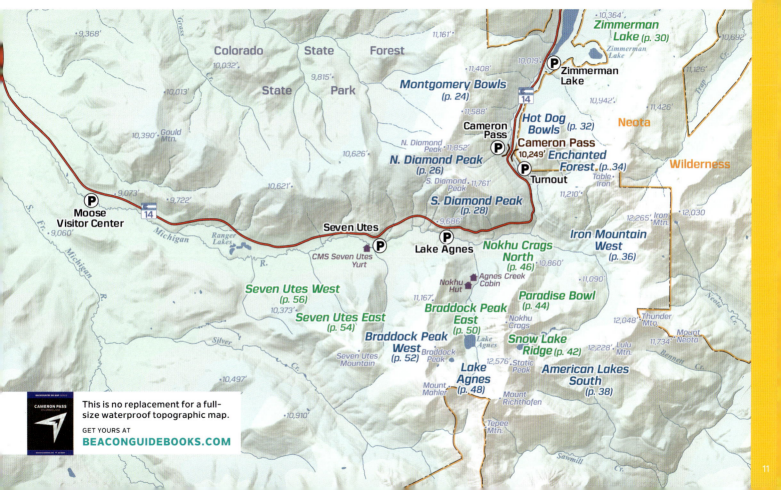

Colorado State Forest

State Park

·10,364'

Zimmerman Lake (p. 30)

10,032'

9,815'

10,013'

·11,161'

·11,408'

10,019'

Zimmerman Lake

10,692'

Zimmerman Lake

·11,126'

14

Montgomery Bowls (p. 24)

·11,588'

Hot Dog Bowls (p. 32)

Neota

·10,390' Gould Mtn.

10,626'

Cameron Pass

Cameron Pass

N. Diamond Peak ·11,852'

10,249' Enchanted Forest (p. 34)

10,942'

·11,426'

Wilderness

N. Diamond Peak (p. 26)

S. Diamond Peak ·11,761'

Turnout

Table Iron

10,621'

·11,210'

·12,030

Moose Visitor Center

9,073'

9,722'

S. Diamond Peak (p. 28)

12,265' Iron Mtn.

9,060'

14

9,686'

Iron Mountain West (p. 36)

Michigan

Ranger Lakes

Seven Utes

Lake Agnes

Nokhu Crags North (p. 46)

·10,860'

·11,090'

12,048'

Thunder Mtn.

Michigan R.

CMS Seven Utes Yurt

Agnes Creek Cabin

Mount Neota

Seven Utes West (p. 56)

Nokhu Hut

11,167'

Paradise Bowl (p. 44)

11,734'

10,373'

Braddock Peak East (p. 50)

Nokhu Crags

Snow Lake Ridge (p. 42)

12,228' Lulu Mtn.

Seven Utes East (p. 54)

Silver

Braddock Peak West (p. 52)

Lake Agnes

American Lakes South (p. 38)

Bennett

Braddock Peak

12,576' Static Peak

Seven Utes Mountain

·10,497'

Lake Agnes (p. 48)

Mount Mahler

·10,910'

Mount Richthofen

Tepee Mtn.

Savmill

CAMERON PASS

This is no replacement for a full-size waterproof topographic map.

GET YOURS AT
BEACONGUIDEBOOKS.COM

11

1 KELLY RIDGE

Clark Peak

North Fork Canadian Yurt

KELLY RIDGE

Viewed from North Park, Colorado, the rampart of the Medicine Bow Range is impressive and continuous. One inconspicuous feature is the ridge immediately west of Kelly Lake. Topping out at over 11,660', this ridge stretches 2 miles with multiple descents to the scattered forests below. The approach is a steep, lengthy skintrack, which explains the relatively few tracks seen on the face. The eastern side of Kelly Ridge has not been explored in the winter, but would yield dramatic (if short) ski runs into the Kelly Lake basin. An ideal basecamp to explore this area is the North Fork Canadian Yurt, operated by Never Summer Nordic.

 As a west-facing slope, Kelly Ridge does not receive the constant wind loading of most Cameron Pass areas. However, be watchful for cross-loaded gullies on the steeper pitches. The windswept ridgeline may present difficult snow conditions for the first several turns.

 Enter State Forest State Park off Colorado Hwy. 14 about 11 miles west of Cameron Pass. (A state parks pass is required beyond this point.) Follow CR 41 for 8 miles to the trailhead at the gated road closure. Restrooms are available.

 Skin out to the North Fork Canadian Yurt, approximately 1.5 miles from the trailhead. Pass the North Fork Canadian Yurt and locate the broad slope south of Mossman Pole Patch Creek. Ascend this slope to the summit or as high as desired.
Alternate Approach: Follow the Kelly Lake summer trail for approximately 3 miles, to the 9,400' contour line. From here, gain the northwest side of Kelly Ridge and climb the occasionally narrow crest. Traverse the rolling ridgeline to the selected descent.

 Upon reaching the valley bottom, ski downstream along the North Fork of the Canadian River to the trailhead.

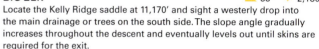

① BIG ELK   38°   2,180'

Locate the Kelly Ridge saddle at 11,170' and sight a westerly drop into the main drainage or trees on the south side. The slope angle gradually increases throughout the descent and eventually levels out until skins are required for the exit.

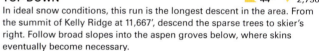

② TOP DOWN   44°   2,790'

In ideal snow conditions, this run is the longest descent in the area. From the summit of Kelly Ridge at 11,667', descend the sparse trees to skier's right. Follow broad slopes into the aspen groves below, where skins eventually become necessary.

③ MAGIC LINE   39°   2,530'

Start from the knob at 11,490' on the southern end of Kelly Ridge. Select a line dropping southwest onto a broad, sparsely wooded slope. Avoid skiing south into the drainage until near the bottom. It is possible to access this from Margy's Knoll, but a lengthy return skintrack will need to be cut.

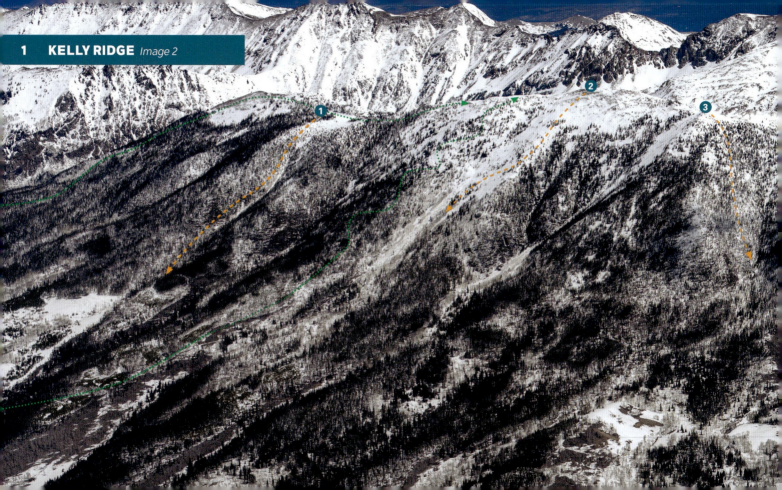

Clark Peak

Siskin

Jewel Lake

Margy's Knoll

Summer Trailhead

RUBY JEWEL CIRQUE

ATES 2

After the installation of Ruby Jewel Yurt in 1985, this area received significant attention from early backcountry skiers (mostly old-school Telemarkers on 3-pin bindings). Three separate drainages can be accessed via the summer jeep road; the area has moderate tree skiing and several couloirs and slopes located at and above timberline.

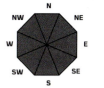

The Ruby Jewel area is a complex snow avalanche environment with a variety of wind and sun aspects. The north-facing slopes remain cold throughout the winter, while easterly aspects tend to be wind-loaded. Expect ridgetops to be wind-scoured.

Enter State Forest State Park off Colorado Hwy. 14 about 11 miles west of Cameron Pass. (A state parks pass is required beyond this point.) Follow CR 41 for 5 miles to the trailhead at the top of a short hill. No facilities are available here.

Skin up the summer jeep road, following occasional blue diamonds to the yurts located along this road. Pass the yurt turn-offs and continue up ever-steeper jeep roads into the selected ski area. There are frequent old logging roads to facilitate your approach to the nearby ridges. **Approach for Margy's Knoll, Jewel Lake Glades, and Little Japan:** The summer jeep road ends at about 10,400'; a closure sign and gate may be visible sticking out of the snow. To summit Margy's Knoll follow the drainage due north for 0.5 mile and bend left (west) to achieve the saddle immediately north of Margy's Knoll. To continue to Ruby Jewel Lake, from the summer closure follow the drainage until it bends right (east) and rises to the open cirque above. Locating Little Japan from the summer road closure requires locating old logging roads trending due east. The logging roads will get you near the 10,850' knoll on Little Japan. **Approach for Lynx Couloirs and Ghost Trees:** At 0.70 miles from Ruby Jewel Yurt there is a sharp curve in the jeep road. From the southernmost point in the curve follow old logging roads onto the north-facing slope. Aim for a gentle knoll at 10,200'. From this knoll proceed steeply uphill and east to the ridgeline at 11,200'.

Return via the skintrack on the main jeep road.

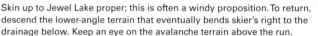
① JEWEL LAKE GLADES   30°   780'

Skin up to Jewel Lake proper; this is often a windy proposition. To return, descend the lower-angle terrain that eventually bends skier's right to the drainage below. Keep an eye on the avalanche terrain above the run.

② LITTLE JAPAN   35°   900'

Using old logging roads, ascend to the knoll at 10,850' and wander up the ridgeline to the east. From your highpoint, descend the ridgeline to the knoll and drop to the north for gladed tree skiing. Managing your elevation loss allows for a traverse to the west and finishes in open trees to the skintrack.

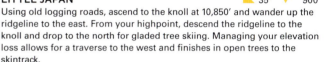
③ MARGY'S KNOLL   39°   550'

Access the summit of Margy's Knoll at 11,000' via a saddle immediately east of the knoll. Sight east down a sparsely treed slope that returns to the skintrack below.

④ GHOST TREES   35°   500'

Seek out old logging roads to top out at 10,800' on the narrow ridge below the entrance to the Lynx Couloirs. Sight a line due west onto a broad slope with numerous dead trees. Eventually, work your way north to return to the skintrack.

⑤ LYNX COULOIRS   45°   800'

After skinning to the high point along the ridge, approach the main couloir on a broad slope at 11,000'. This slope rapidly constricts to a rock-walled chute before spilling into open slopes below.

Clark Peak

CLARK PEAK

Skiing this area requires a lengthy approach, starting with 2 miles of flat road skiing. For those willing to make the effort, the upper bowls of Clark Peak offer dramatic alpine skiing with few other skiers. The skiing above timberline can be challenging due to wind-affected snow, but once below timberline, snowed-in trees and glades lead toward Fall Creek.

 As the highest peak in the Medicine Bow Range, Clark Peak (12,951') gathers significant snow with wind-loaded slopes. Be aware of cross-loaded slopes. Expect to encounter a thin snowpack just below the ridgelines.

 Park at the Blue Lake trailhead along Hwy.14. If the parking lot is full, the Long Draw parking lot, 200 yards to the north, makes a good substitute. There are no restrooms at Blue Lake trailhead.

 Use the summer trail to Blue Lake to approach for the first 2 miles. At this point, the summer trail crosses Fall Creek on a prominent footbridge and veers left on unmarked trails heading to Blue Lake. Find an opportunity to leave the trail and proceed westerly uphill into the basin.

Alternative Approach to Sacred Trees: Approximately 0.3 miles before the Blue Lake Trail crosses Fall Creek on the prominent footbridge, locate an old logging road switchbacking to the west on the ridge. Follow this ridge to the summit of Sacred Trees at 11,200' and select your line.

 Return directly to the skintrack approach. If time and conditions permit, extend the day with an ascent to a saddle at 11,000' near the top of the Sacred Trees run and return via the Sawmill Creek drainage.

 COOK CITY 37° 2,250'

From the south summit of Clark Peak, descend broad slopes to the basin below. Snow and avalanche conditions may require you to start your descent below the summit. Eventually, lower-angle terrain drops back to Fall Creek and the return skintrack. Alternatively, at 11,000', a short skintrack crosses into Sawmill Creek from the south.

SACRED TREES 30° 1,200'

From the ridgetop at 11,200', scout the trees dropping north into Fall Creek. There are brief steep pitches near timberline. Clever route-finding pieces together tree runs for over a thousand vertical feet. Some of the lower slopes were burned in the 2020 Cameron Peak Fire, making for interesting skiing between burned snags.

 Blue *does not mean this area is like a blue square run at the ski resort. Blue means "challenging avalanche terrain." Learn more about the ATES scale on page 9.*

Parkview Mountain

Chickadee

Junco

Siskin

SAWMILL CREEK

The Sawmill Creek drainage offers a rugged backcountry experience despite a relatively easy approach. At the end of the drainage, the five craggy points, locally known as the Bird Peaks, are all above 12,000'. The lower half of this area was clear-cut in the 1960s; remnants of logging roads abound in this area. Higher up, the drainage enters the Rawah Wilderness—and a more pristine forest.

 The entire Sawmill ridgeline faces due east, which leads to significant wind-loaded slopes. The colder north-facing aspects often develop multiple faceted layers.

 Park at the Blue Lake trailhead along Hwy. 14, across from the Long Draw Road turnoff (closed in winter to vehicles, but open to snowmobiles). Walk or ski 0.25 miles south along the road to the faintly marked and gated road on the right into Sawmill Creek.

 Skin up the gradual jeep road to a fork at 1.5 miles. By the time the distant peaks come into view it will be obvious that the upper Sawmill drainage is large and complex. Carefully navigate left or right to the runs of interest and look for access to the ridgeline for the final approach. In favorable snow conditions, it is feasible to bootpack to the summits.

 Once the steep skiing is over, follow the original skintrack back to the road. Although flat for some sections, most skiers will continue down without skins, instead utilizing double-poling and skating.

❶ THE BIRD 45° ▼ 950'
From the high point known as Siskin at 12,400', select the main couloir dropping back into the basin.

❷ DAVE'S WAY 43° ▼ 1,120'
From the high point known as Junco at 12,385', scope out the prominent bowl descending back into Sawmill basin.

❸ WILD BLUE 50° ▼ 1,000'
After topping out at 12,169' on the point known as Chickadee, sight down the north face. Select the least wind-affected couloir for the descent.

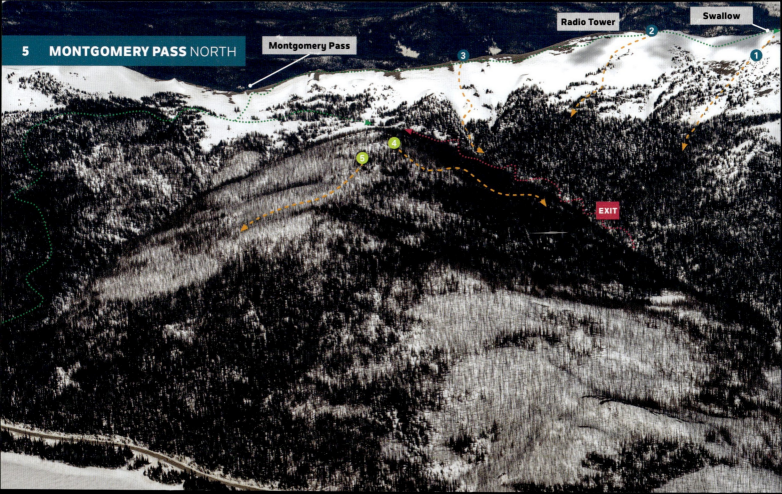

Montgomery Pass

Radio Tower

Swallow

EXIT

MONTGOMERY PASS NORTH

Often used as an alternative to the more crowded ski/ride scene of the Montgomery Bowls, this sector offers many descents from the ridgeline down easterly aspects. Immediately east of the ridgeline sits the high point locally known as The Pimple (10,990'), which offers tree glades off the north side.

The rolling ridgeline profile north of Montgomery Pass frequently produces wind-loaded slopes. The terrain convexities tend to encourage the formation of dangerous wind slabs. These are not obvious from above and ought to be identified before dropping in. Approach with caution.

Park at the large Zimmerman Lake trailhead, 1.5 miles north of Cameron Pass. This parking lot is frequently crowded on weekends. Restroom facilities are available. Cross Hwy. 14 to the northwest and locate the well-marked Montgomery Pass trail.

Skin up the well-used trail. At the 1.25 mile mark, take the right-hand fork towards Montgomery Pass. Continue north until the open slopes north of Montgomery Pass become visible. Stay on the ridgeline proper (conditions permitting) or traverse to The Pimple.

Returning via the approach trail is viable, but be aware of uphill travelers on the descent. An optional descent is to use Scar Face Run to return to the lower portion of the approach trail.

1 MAXWELL HOUSE TREES  30° ▼ 1,200'

Gain the point known as Swallow at 11,640'. Depending on snow conditions, choose a line that drops east through the sparse trees into the North Fork of Joe Wright Creek.

2 RADIO TOWER 36° ▼ 1,100'

Depending on snow cover, there are several broad, sweeping runs off the ridgeline north of Montgomery Pass. The farther north the starting spot, the greater the run length. A radio telemetry tower at 11,500' marks the logical high spot.

3 JULES   27° ▼ 600'

From approximately 11,300' along the ridgeline, choose a slope descending easterly into a drainage. Tighter tree skiing below timberline terminates in the creek drainage.

4 DROP ZONE 22° ▼ 700'

The Pimple's north side offers several tree-gladed runs dropping into the creek at the bottom. Multiple versions exist to explore.

5 SCAR FACE 27° ▼ 700'

From the summit of The Pimple, traverse easterly onto the broad, fire-scarred slope. The farther skier's left you travel, the lower in Montgomery Creek you'll reach. Skin back to the Montgomery Pass Trail or plunge ahead to Hwy. 14.

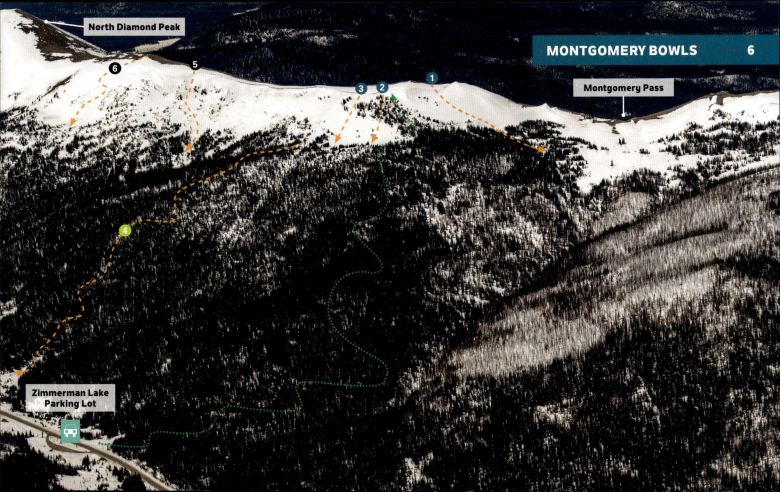

North Diamond Peak

Montgomery Pass

Zimmerman Lake
Parking Lot

MONTGOMERY BOWLS

The most popular, easy-to-access sector on Cameron Pass is the Montgomery Bowls area, not to be confused with Montgomery Pass itself. The Montgomery Bowls feature trees that reach to the ridgeline and collect plentiful snow in low-risk avalanche terrain. For more serious descents and steeper runs, move south along the ridgeline.

The ridgeline immediately above the Montgomery Bowls develops cornices throughout the winter, and wind-loaded slopes below are common. Far skier's right, the runs enter complex avalanche terrain.

Park at the large Zimmerman Lake trailhead, approximately 1.5 miles north of Cameron Pass. This parking lot is frequently crowded on weekends. Restroom facilities are available. Cross Hwy. 14 to the northwest and locate the well-marked Montgomery Pass Trail.

Skin up the well-used trail. At the 1.25 mile mark, take the left-hand fork, which rises steeply to the base of Montgomery Bowls. From here, a skintrack on looker's right climbs to the ridgeline.

 Return via the approach trail, which can be icy and fast; be aware of uphill travelers. An optional descent is Explorer's Glades, although skins are needed to return to Hwy. 14.

1 MR. BIG   30° 350'

After gaining the ridgeline above Montgomery Bowl, travel north on the windswept ground and select a line on the broad slope. Continuing through the trees below will put you on the Montgomery Pass North approach skintrack.

2 MONTGOMERY BOWL LEFT   30° 300'

The approach skintrack usually ends just at timberline. The last bit of elevation isn't worth the effort unless the ridgeline is the objective. From immediately below the ridgeline, choose from any number of options leading to the bottom. The short approach lends itself to multiple laps. This is probably the most skied slope on Cameron Pass—expect to see other skiers/riders.

3 MONTGOMERY BOWL RIGHT   30° 350'

Move skier's right as far as conditions allow and choose from multiple lines dropping to the bottom. The avalanche risk increases with each move south, so be prepared to assess the risk frequently.

4 EXPLORER'S GLADES   25° 880'

A low-angle, low-avalanche-risk option, Explorer's Glades is often used as an alternative return to Hwy. 14. Piece together variable trees and glades for the descent. Remember, a short skin back to the road is required.

5 COOKIE CUTTER CHUTES   45° 525'

From the prominent high point at 11,588', locate steep chutes on the NE aspect. Choose any well-covered gully for a quick drop to the trees. Continue down to Hwy. 14 or traverse skier's left to Montgomery Bowls.

6 EAST FACE OF POINT 11,588 40° 800'

The broad east face of high point 11,588' drops directly into the forest below. Continue through steep trees to Hwy. 14 or traverse skier's left to Montgomery Bowls.

Cameron Pass Trailhead

NORTH DIAMOND PEAK

ATES 2

The North Diamond Peak sector sees less ski traffic than the nearby areas, even though the snow and terrain are arguably as good. Descent from the summit of North Diamond places the skier into steep trees, which can be skied down to Hwy. 14. Alternatively, by holding a high traverse, it's possible to return to the South Diamond exit routes.

As an east-facing bowl, North Diamond Peak frequently develops wind-loaded slopes. The cornices along the ridgeline can trigger larger slides below.

Park at the Cameron Pass summit, a 65-mile drive up Poudre Canyon from Fort Collins. The summit parking lot for Cameron Pass is crowded on most days and not always well plowed. Park carefully to maximize available spots. Restrooms are available.

Skin directly up behind the restrooms (hence the local name of Outhouse Gully). The upper half of this gully is part of the runout path of South Diamond. Use discretion to avoid this exposure. Continue up the looker's right skintrack to the ridgeline. From the ridgeline, head north to North Diamond.

Continue down North Diamond Trees run to exit near the parking lot; skins may be necessary. Alternatively, a high traverse provides access to the South Diamond exit.

① WHISKEY RIVER 33° ▽ 1,520'

From the summit of North Diamond Peak (11,857'), drop directly into the broad, east-facing bowl. Follow the natural drainage to the bottom for tree skiing nearly to the trailhead parking lot.

② THE WEASEL 32° 600'

Starting just south of the North Diamond summit, take the broad, lower-angle slope to the flats. Bear to the left to finish in North Diamond Trees or traverse right back to the South Diamond exit.

③ NORTH DIAMOND TREES 24° 800'

These moderately spaced trees make for a reasonable descent from North Diamond Peak. Near the bottom, veer skier's right to arrive near the trailhead.

What is ATES?

Green, Blue and Black in our books and maps DO NOT identify a difficulty rating. The Avalanche Terrain Exposure Scale is used to identify the type and level of avalanche exposure a particular zone contains. See page 9 for more information.

Mount Mahler

Braddock Peak

To Walden

Cameron Pass Trailhead

ATES 2

SOUTH DIAMOND PEAK

South Diamond Peak is the towering symbol of backcountry skiing and riding at Cameron Pass. The entire east face dominates the highway view for the last mile when approaching from Fort Collins. This area attracts significant attention for the quick access and dramatic runs.

The consistent slope angle, combined with frequent wind loading, creates a perfect storm of avalanche risk. As of January 2022, five avalanche deaths and numerous complete burials have occurred here. Existing ski tracks are no measure of avalanche risk. In June 1995, an avalanche encompassing the entire east face of South Diamond Peak flowed into the summit parking lot.

Park at the Cameron Pass summit, a 65-mile drive up Poudre Canyon from Fort Collins. The summit parking lot for Cameron Pass is crowded on most days and not always well plowed. Park carefully to maximize available spots. Restrooms are available.

Skin directly up behind the restrooms (hence the local name of Outhouse Gully). The upper half of this gully is in the runout path of South Diamond; use discretion to avoid this exposure. Continue up the looker's right skintrack to the ridgeline and south to summit South Diamond Peak at 11,700'.

Optional Approach: Traverse left from the Cameron Pass parking lot and diagonally approach the south shoulder of South Diamond Peak. To minimize avalanche exposure, avoid the steep slopes under the Taster's Choice run.

EXIT

Return to the trailhead via one of many open runout zones below the main face.

① PTARMIGAN FACE 38° ▼ 500'

The broad slope skier's left of the summit is the quintessential backcountry ski run of Northern Colorado. The snow on this slope is consistently good; this is the run most frequently skied on South Diamond Peak.

② MAIN FACE 40° ▼ 675'

From the summit of South Diamond Peak, descend the broad slope. Choose a left or right option near the bottom to avoid rocky cliffs.

③ THE GASH 43° ▼ 600'

Slightly skier's right of the summit, seek out a gully which narrows near the bottom. The old name of "avalanche alley" is appropriate.

④ THE WAVE 39° ▼ 450'

The slope skier's right of The Gash follows a sweeping line to the flats below. Locally, this is known as the area most likely to avalanche.

⑤ PABST 37° ▼ 375'

The original naming history of this run is unclear, but it is certainly Pabst, after the popular red-white-and-blue beer. Over time the name morphed into "Pap Smear"; this atlas chooses to retain the original name. Pabst is the last slope before entering the Taster's Choice trees; this run offers a quick drop to the bottom on a relatively narrow slope.

⑥ TASTER'S CHOICE 37° ▼ 350'

When trees are on the menu, Taster's Choice delivers. Seek modest shots between steeply set trees. Avalanches have started and run through these trees.

Comanche Peak

3 2

Zimmerman Lake

EXIT

To Fort Collins

Zimmerman Lake Trailhead

ZIMMERMAN LAKE

Zimmerman Lake is a popular destination for cross-country skiing and snowshoeing. But beyond the lake are numerous low-angle backcountry ski options for those willing to approach the north side of Iron Mountain. This windswept sector offers several slopes, gullies, and high mountain traverses.

The forested, low-angle slopes above Zimmerman Lake significantly reduce the avalanche risk in this sector. Above timberline, wind-loaded slopes are common.

Park at the large Zimmerman Lake trailhead, approximately 1.5 miles north of Cameron Pass. This parking lot is frequently crowded on weekends. Restroom facilities are available.

Skin 2 miles up the old jeep road to Zimmerman Lake at 10,500'. Proceed around the skier's left side of the lake on a cross-country trail. On the far side of the lake, leave the trail and angle northeast to an area known as the Iron Mountain Pinnacles at 10,800'.

Navigate back to Zimmerman Lake. There are several options to return to Zimmerman Lake, not all involve returning to the ascent skintrack. See exit options drawn on the photo.

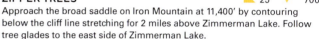

① ZIPPER TREES   25°   700'

Approach the broad saddle on Iron Mountain at 11,400' by contouring below the cliff line stretching for 2 miles above Zimmerman Lake. Follow tree glades to the east side of Zimmerman Lake.

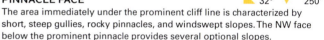

② PINNACLE FACE   32°   250'

The area immediately under the prominent cliff line is characterized by short, steep gullies, rocky pinnacles, and windswept slopes. The NW face below the prominent pinnacle provides several optional slopes.

③ ALLY   33°   350'

Negotiate the rocky valley behind the Iron Mountain Pinnacle. Some walking may be necessary. Watch for a narrow gully descending NE into the forest below. Ski the gully or ridge immediately skier's left, depending on snow conditions. Return to Zimmerman Lake by proceeding west to reach the Meadows XC ski trail.

Green does not mean it's "easy". Green means "simple avalanche terrain". Learn more about the ATES scale on page 9.

10 HOT DOG BOWLS

Diamond Peaks

Zimmerman Lake

HOT DOG BOWLS

These bowls occupy a sheltered spot tucked in behind the most northern remnants of the Never Summer Range. The bowls offer modest glade skiing on the east side, gradually, steepening to the west where more challenging and avalanche prone terrain lies. Good tree skiing for the adventurous drops directly off the north end.

 The deceptively short runs on Hot Dog Bowls hide the presence of wind-loaded slopes with north-facing facet layers. Use caution when approaching and descending.

 Park at the large Zimmerman Lake trailhead, approximately 1.5 miles north of Cameron Pass. This parking lot is frequently crowded on weekends. Restroom facilities are available.

 Start up the trail to Zimmerman Lake from the southeast end of the parking lot. Immediately after entering the trees, turn right into thick trees, cross the small, unnamed drainage, and skin SE to the base of the bowls.
Optional Approach: Shortly after leaving the Zimmerman Lake Trail, proceed up a consistently steep skin track directly towards the Big Mac run. At the base of Big Mac, the terrain is flat and open; negotiate the slope above to the top at 11,350'.

 The best return follows the approach skintrack. Avoid dropping all the way into the flat creek drainage up higher in the basin.

① HOT DOG EAST   26°   300'

Far skier's right in the Hot Dog Bowls is moderate terrain that offers several options dropping into glades below.

② HOT DOG WEST   32°   400'

The steep couloirs and bowls on skier's left of the Hot Dog Bowls offer broad slopes or tight gullies.

③ BIG MAC   35°   400'

A steep option to avoid the rocky chutes near Hot Dog West is to hug the ridgeline immediately skier's left of the dropoff. Rocky knolls and short, steep drops lead into steep tree skiing before leveling out.

④ HAMBURGER TREES   23°   1,100'

This run can be started from the most northerly point of the Hot Dog Bowls area, but the snow is often wind-affected here. Regardless of the starting point, choose a descent through glades and occasionally tight trees to the skintrack. To connect to the approach skintrack, trend skier's right near the bottom.

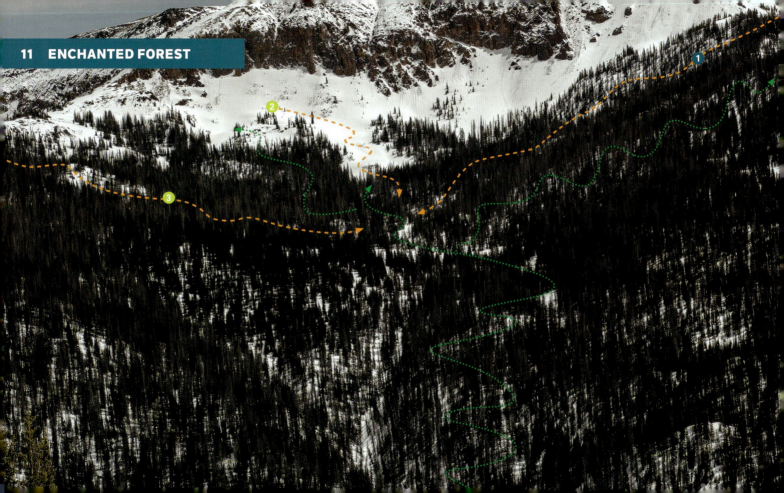

ENCHANTED FOREST

The Enchanted Forest offers a welcome change from the more crowded Diamond Peaks area. This broad, bowl-shaped basin offers skiing on most aspects for a variety of snow and terrain options. The most traveled aspect is the south side of the bowl, where it tucks up against the imposing cliffs of Iron Mountain.

This sector's complex wind and sun angles make evaluating avalanche risk challenging. The avalanche risk can vary subtly with aspect changes. Pay attention to which slopes are mentioned in the avalanche report for the day.

Park at a slow vehicle turnout 0.5 miles south of the Cameron Pass summit. There is room for only a few vehicles here and no facilities. Other slow vehicle turnouts below this point are signed "No Parking."

Skin directly east uphill to gain the Michigan Ditch. Turn right (south) and follow the ditch for 0.3 miles. Watch for a skintrack on the left, immediately after a pronounced curve in the ditch. Skin steeply for 400' until the terrain levels out in the basin.

Return via your original skintrack. Avoid the steep-sided terrain trap gully immediately to the north.

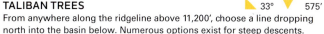

① TALIBAN TREES 33° 575'

From anywhere along the ridgeline above 11,200', choose a line dropping north into the basin below. Numerous options exist for steep descents.

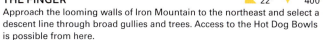

② THE FINGER 22° 400'

Approach the looming walls of Iron Mountain to the northeast and select a descent line through broad gullies and trees. Access to the Hot Dog Bowls is possible from here.

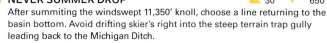

③ NEVER SUMMER DROP 30° 650'

After summiting the windswept 11,350' knoll, choose a line returning to the basin bottom. Avoid drifting skier's right into the steep terrain trap gully leading back to the Michigan Ditch.

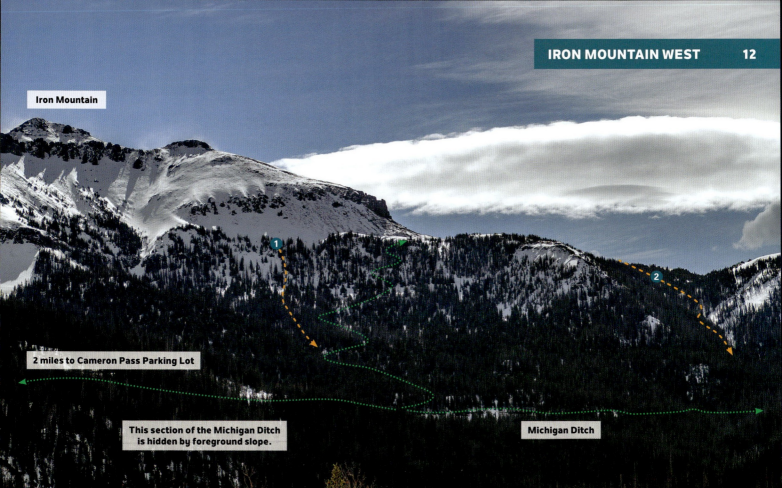

Iron Mountain

2 miles to Cameron Pass Parking Lot

This section of the Michigan Ditch
is hidden by foreground slope.

Michigan Ditch

IRON MOUNTAIN WEST

In the early 20th century, it was widely believed that Iron Mountain was the remnants of an ancient caldera. While these rocks have been influenced by igneous geologic activity, they are not actual volcanic cliffs. The broad, forested slopes of west Iron Mountain were heavily logged fifty years ago, providing numerous old roads that lead to timberline. The drainages and gullies tend to offer the best snow, but sparsely treed slopes can be skied all the way to the Michigan Ditch.

As a west-facing slope, this sector has fewer wind-loaded slopes than across the highway on South Diamond. However, be aware of cross-loaded gullies and slopes.

The most straightforward access is to park at the Enchanted Trees slow vehicle turnout, 0.5 miles west of the Cameron Pass summit.

Skin directly east up to the Michigan Ditch. Follow the ditch south for 1.9 miles until old logging roads provide uphill skinning onto the west side of Iron Mountain.

Return along the Michigan Ditch.

❶ IRON MOUNTAIN GLADES  35° 1,000'
After negotiating logging roads as high as possible, select a descent through steep trees and occasional glades to Michigan Ditch.

❷ LUCY'S DRAW 37° 850'
Use a number of possible skintrack approaches to gain the saddle at 11,250' between Iron Mountain and Thunder Mountain. Enjoy the consistent angle and scattered tree skiing to Michigan Ditch.

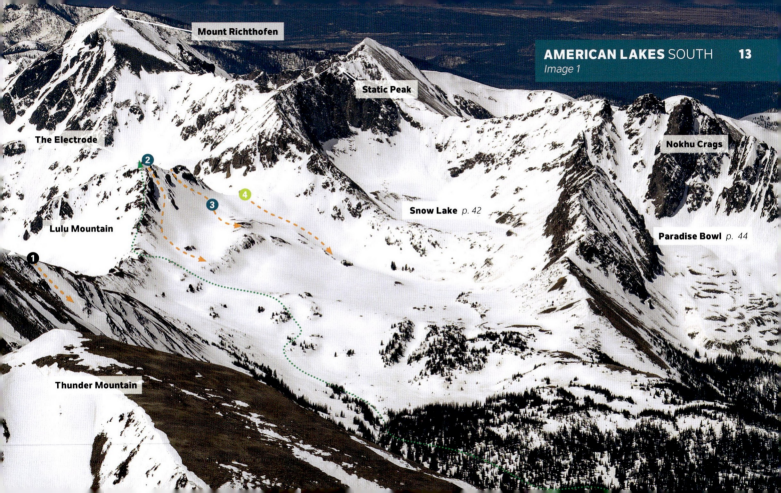

Mount Richthofen

Static Peak

The Electrode

Nokhu Crags

Lulu Mountain

Snow Lake *p. 42*

Paradise Bowl *p. 44*

Thunder Mountain

2

AMERICAN LAKES SOUTH

The long approach makes this the best snowmobile-assisted ski option in State Forest State Park. Expect to see recreational snowmobilers in this area. For skiers, the snowmobile trail is the quickest approach into the final sweeping bowl dominated by Thunder Mountain, Lulu Mountain, and Static Peak. Adventurous skiers can drop south from Thunder Pass into Rocky Mountain National Park for a few laps before returning to the snowmobile trail exit. Note: Snowmobiles are not permitted in Rocky Mountain

This vast, open cirque contains many avalanche-prone slopes. Evaluate runs carefully after reviewing the avalanche forecast.

Use the Lake Agnes winter parking lot, located 2.5 miles west of Cameron Pass. A state parks pass is required to park here. No facilities are available.

Follow the summer road due east on a snowmobile route and continue for 2.6 miles to the Michigan Ditch. Cross the ditch and continue for 2 miles, using the snowmobile trail until above timberline. Above timberline, climb north onto Thunder Pass to access Lulu Mountain or The Electrode.

Return via the snowmobile trail.

The American Lakes area is popular with recreational snowmobilers and sled-assisted skiers. Most snowmobiles access this area from the Seven Utes Parking Lot. The snowmobile trail is groomed up to the Michigan Ditch, above here the trail is ungroomed and can be challenging to ride. Snowmobiles are not allowed on the Michigan Ditch.

❶ LULU'S LEMONS 44° 1,250'

Approach the summit of Lulu Mountain via Thunder Pass, or, to better assess the snowpack, bootpack directly up the north couloir. The most prominent gully presents the ideal descent. Westerly winds often strip this run of soft snow until spring conditions settle the snowpack.

❷ EDISON 44° 500'

The north face of The Electrode presents a steep slope trending to skier's right. Descend to the basin below.

❸ TESLA 40° 350'

From the low, westerly saddle of The Electrode, sight a straightforward slope into the basin below.

❹ LOW VOLTAGE 25° 300'

The low-angle saddle between The Electrode and Static Peak offers smooth bowl skiing. This bowl also provides access via steep chutes south into Rocky Mountain National Park. Snowmobile-assisted skiers and riders use this area frequently.

Lulu Mountain

①

Thunder Pass

WESTERN
COLORADO UNIVERSITY

PARTNERSHIP PROGRAM
COMPUTER SCIENCE & ENGINEERING

ENGINEERING THE FUTURE OF ADVENTURE

University of Colorado
Boulder

Nokhu Crags

The Electrode

Snow Lake

Seven Dwarfs Area

1

2

SNOW LAKE RIDGE

ATES 2

The long approach makes this the best snowmobile-assisted ski option in State Forest State Park. Expect to see recreational snowmobilers in this area. For skiers, the snowmobile trail is the quickest approach into the final sweeping bowl dominated by Thunder Mountain, Lulu Mountain, and Static Peak.

The south side of Snow Lake ridgeline can develop wind-loaded slopes from westerly winds. Late in the ski season, the southerly exposure requires spring avalanche assessment.

Use the Lake Agnes winter parking lot, located 2.5 miles west of Cameron Pass. A state parks pass is required to park here. No facilities are available.

Follow the summer road due east on a snowmobile route and continue for 2.6 miles to the Michigan Ditch. Cross the ditch and continue 2 miles using the snowmobile trail until above timberline. All the Dwarf couloirs are best approached by climbing directly up the chosen run.

The best approach to Snow White is to ascend the Nokhouloir from Paradise Bowl. See Nokhouloir on the next page.

Return via the snowmobile trail.

The American Lakes area is popular with recreational snowmobilers and sled-assisted skiers. Most snowmobiles access this area from the Seven Utes Parking Lot. The snowmobile trail is groomed up to the Michigan Ditch, above here the trail is ungroomed and can be challenging to ride. Snowmobiles are not allowed on the Michigan Ditch.

❶ SNOW WHITE 48° 850'

Choose an approach to the south summit of the Nokhu Crags at 12,400'. Locate the broad, south-facing slope that starts from the summit and descends directly to Snow Lake.

❷ SEVEN DWARFS AREA 50° 350'

The Seven Dwarfs are a series of short, steep couloirs along the ridgeline that extends easterly from the south summit of Nokhu Crags. While descending directly from the ridge is possible, it may be prudent to bootpack the approach to discern the exact line and snow conditions.

ATES ratings and avalanche bulletins must be used together for evaluating hazards and managing personal risk in the backcountry. Learn more about the ATES scale on page 9.

Seven Utes Mountain

Static Peak

Snow Lake

PARADISE BOWL

ATES 3

The Nokhu Crags were locally called Sawtooth Crags until the 1920s. The current name is believed to derive from the Arapaho word for "Eagles Nest." The name Nokhu Crags appears on maps from 1900. The east side of the Nokhu Crags offers exciting and accessible backcountry runs for skiers and riders. The eastern cirque towers over 1,000 feet; be cautious of the loose rock. At least one fatality has occurred scrambling on the upper towers. The most impressive features are the steep couloirs concentrated in the NE headwall of the Nokhu Crags. Less committing bowls, glades, and trees can be found on other aspects.

 This tight cirque has a multitude of avalanche hazards. Wind-loaded slopes are common on all aspects, and the north-facing terrain promotes a weak, faceted snowpack. In the spring, loose avalanches often bring down rockfall in the couloirs.

 Use the Lake Agnes winter parking lot, located 2.5 miles west of Cameron Pass. A state parks pass is required to park here. No facilities are available.

 Ski directly east out of the parking lot and follow the snowmobile trail for 0.6 miles. Bear south, cross the bridge, and ski uphill for 0.2 miles. Watch for a diagonal access road angling left and up. Note: this access road crosses two major avalanche paths. Follow the road to the Michigan Ditch and continue directly up the drainage into Paradise Bowl.

 Return via the approach track.

❶ BREAKFAST COULOIR
 50° ▼ 300'

Descend the short, steep couloir at the far south end of the cirque. The most obvious ascent is to bootpack the gully.

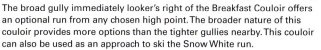

❷ NOKHOULOIR
 52° ▼ 700'

The broad gully immediately looker's right of the Breakfast Couloir offers an optional run from any chosen high point. The broader nature of this couloir provides more options than the tighter gullies nearby. This couloir can also be used as an approach to ski the Snow White run.

❸ GRAND CENTRAL COULOIR
 55° ▼ 700'

This striking couloir is not visible until directly under the Nokhu Crags east face. Steep and continuous, it offers a challenging ascent as well as descent. The notoriously loose rock of the crags is a common hazard.

❹ THREE SISTERS
60° ▼ 600'

While approaching the headwall of the Paradise Bowl, it is impossible not to notice the three narrow couloirs looming above. Bootpack as high as feasible for a rapid drop onto the broad slope below. At least one avalanche fatality has occurred below these slopes.

❺ SHORT BOI
 38° ▼ 580'

This run can be approached via the rolling ridgeline from the northeast. Descend the broad slope from the notch in the ridgeline at 11,550'. This run provides an optional return from the American Lakes area back to the Michigan Ditch.

❻ NOKHU GLADES
 28° ▼ 500'

A variety of glade and tree options descend from the ridge above the skintrack. The farther skier's left you start, the longer the run.

NOKHU CRAGS NORTH

Next to South Diamond, this area is the most impressive face of Cameron Pass when viewed from the highway. The west side is thoroughly scoured by wind and rarely holds sufficient snow to interest skiers. But the north-facing side reveals steep chutes that offer long, continuous ski runs.

 The steep, north-facing prow creates complex avalanche conditions, including wind slabs and deep facet layers. Avalanches here have fully buried skiers.

 Use the Lake Agnes winter parking lot, located 2.5 miles west of Cameron Pass. A state parks pass is required to park here. No facilities are available.

 Ski directly east out of the parking lot and follow the snowmobile trail for 0.6 miles. Bear south, cross the bridge, and ski uphill for 0.2 miles. Watch for an access road angling left and up. Note: This access road crosses two major avalanche paths. Follow the road to the Michigan Ditch. After crossing the ditch, locate logging roads leading to the ridgeline at 10,800'.

 Drop all the way to the Michigan River for access to the snowmobile trail back to the trailhead.

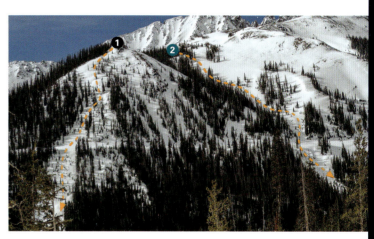

❶ THE LONGEST RUN 42° 1,075'
Drop off the knoll at 10,800' and descend the steep couloir for a continuous run. While technically not the longest run on Cameron Pass, this is a challenging continuous descent.

❷ SHANTY RUN 33° 900'
A prominent gully 100 yards south of the knoll leads into a narrowing slope that ultimately crosses the Michigan Ditch and arrives near the summer Crags Campground.

ATES 3

S

EXIT

N NE E SE S SW W NW

 (avalanche icon)

 S (parking icon)

 (route icon)

 EXIT

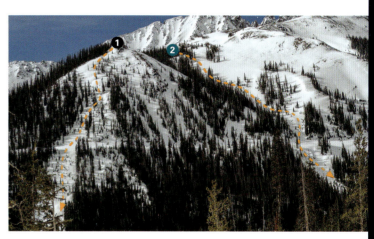 (photo of Nokhu Crags with marked ski routes 1 and 2)

 (slope angle icon)

 (vertical drop icon)

 (compass rose showing N NE E SE S SW W NW)

 (parking S icon)

 (mountain/avalanche icon)

 (ATES 3 icon)

 (EXIT icon)

 (route/approach icon)

 (vertical feet icon)

 (degree icon)

 (compass)

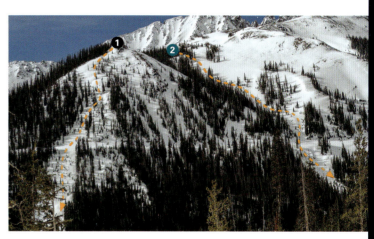 (main photo)

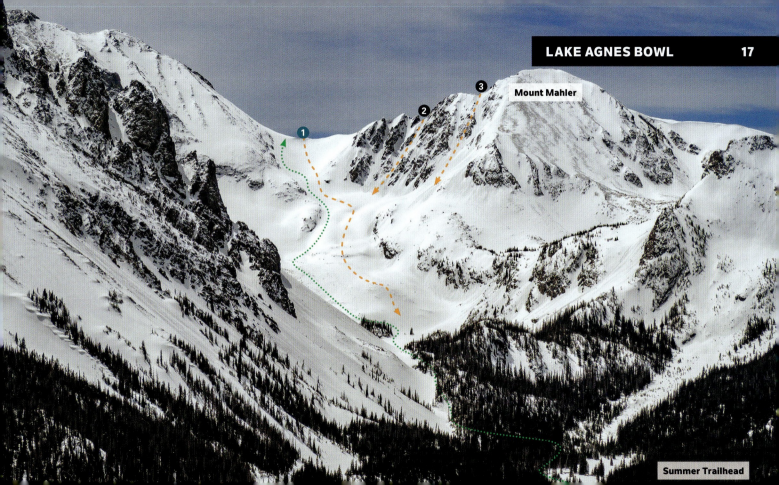

Mount Mahler

Summer Trailhead

LAKE AGNES BOWL

ATES 3

Lake Agnes was named for the youngest daughter of John Zimmerman, an early European immigrant to the area. According to Ansel Watrous' 1910 book *A History of Larimer County*, this lake was believed to be the crater of a recently dormant volcano. The lengthy approach limits the winter use of the beautiful cirque above Lake Agnes. Flanked by the Nokhu Crags, Static Peak, Mount Richthofen, Mount Mahler, and Braddock Peak, the view is a remarkable sight. When the summer road opens in late June, these mountains offer great spring skiing.

Like all high mountain cirques, the Lake Agnes Bowl contains a number of dangerous avalanche features, including cornices and wind-loaded slopes.

Use the Lake Agnes winter parking lot, located 2.5 miles west of Cameron Pass. A state parks pass is required to park here. No facilities are available.

Ski directly east out of the parking lot and follow the snowmobile trail for 0.6 miles. Bear south, cross the bridge, and ski the summer road 1.5 miles to the Lake Agnes summer trailhead. When the road is open in late June, it is possible to drive to the end of the road.

EXIT Return directly to Lake Agnes. The lake is much easier to skirt on the east side when hiking.

1 FOURTH OF JULY BOWL 38° 450'

This iconic snow bowl, tucked into a tight mountain cirque, is visible from Hwy. 14. From the saddle at 12,000', ride the broad slopes to Lake Agnes. Spring skiing here lasts into July each year.

2 X COULOIR 50° 600'

The first and shortest of two couloir lines off Mount Mahler, the X Couloir demands precise skiing. Access via the ridgeline is possible, but bootpacking up the gully is practical in stable snow conditions.

3 Y COULOIR 55° 700'

The Y Couloir is the steepest line on Mount Mahler; ideal snow conditions are critical. Timing your descent well is imperative. Sluff avalanches here are often mixed with loose rock.

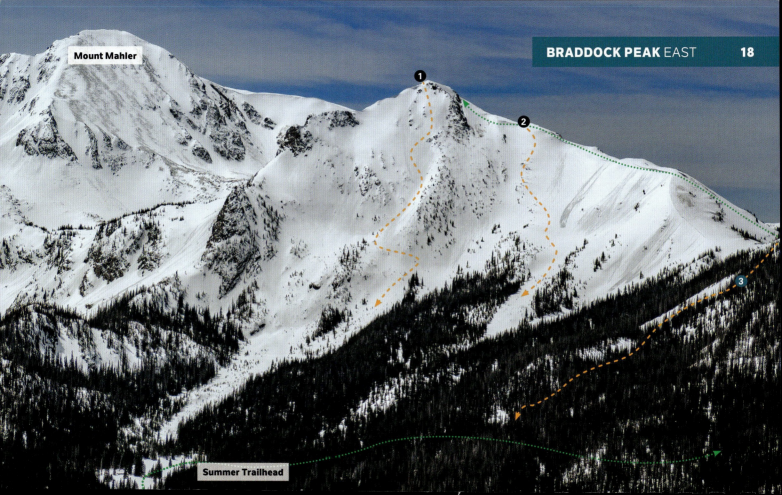

Mount Mahler

Summer Trailhead

ATES 2

BRADDOCK PEAK EAST

Dominating the west side of the Lake Agnes area, this peak is best ascended by its north ridge, accessed by piecing together old logging roads. Under ideal snow conditions, the slopes can be bootpacked to the summit. The premier line is the Z Couloir, which drops from the summit directly to the summer trailhead.

Steep, wind-loaded slopes dominate Braddock Peak. Historic avalanche paths drop to the valley bottom.

Use the Lake Agnes winter parking lot, located 2.5 miles west of Cameron Pass. A state parks pass is required to park here. No facilities are available.

Ski directly east out of the parking lot and follow the snowmobile trail for 0.6 miles. Bear south, cross the bridge, and ski the summer road 1.5 miles to the Lake Agnes summer trailhead. When the road is open in late June, it is possible to drive to the end of the road.

The runs on this side of the mountain all return to the valley bottom near the skintrack.

 Z COULOIR   40°   1,200'

The natural line of the Z Couloir is best appreciated in late spring when the surrounding terrain becomes snow-free. In winter, approach the summit of Braddock Peak via the north ridge, but in spring conditions, bootpacking the couloir is practical. Over 1,000' of tight couloir skiing opens to the slopes below.

 BRADDOCK FACE   43°   800'

The broad slope of Braddock Peak's east face provides a number of descent possibilities. In places, the face is steeper than the Z Couloir. Finish through scattered trees to the valley bottom.

❸ AGNES GLADES   35°   900'

The north ridge of Braddock Peak offers several spots where steep trees and glades drop to the basin below.

Seven Utes Trailhead

BRADDOCK PEAK WEST

The west side of Braddock Peak includes several challenging runs into the drainage east of Seven Utes Mountain. While the upper reaches are often wind-scoured, the trees below hold good snow with gladed tree runs. Three prominent gullies form a large "W" on the forested slope and are known as the Wolf Gullies.

ATES 2

Frequent high winds make for wind-loaded slopes, especially across gullies.

Park at the large Seven Utes parking lot, located 4 miles west of Cameron Pass; this is inside the State Forest State Park and a state parks pass is required. This lot is also used by snowmobiles accessing the American Lakes area. The Colorado Mountain School maintains the Seven Utes Yurt at this location.

Approaching the east side of Seven Utes requires careful map reading. Skin southeast out of the parking lot and immediately drop to the Michigan River. Cross a small bridge and continue south on the steepening trail. After intersecting the snowmobile road, turn left and continue steeply up the first two switchbacks. Watch for a vague trail heading due south from the snowmobile trail. Follow this faint track for 1 mile, then seek a steep skintrack on the east side of the valley to timberline. This sector can also be approached from Braddock Peak's northern ridgeline via the Lake Agnes trailhead.

Most skiers return via the ascent track, which entails some slightly uphill sections.

① WOLF 32° 1,200'

This is the northernmost run of the Wolf Gullies. From the high point at 11,188' along the north ridge of Braddock Peak, sight a drop west into the broad slope that soon narrows into a tree lined gully. Follow this to the creek drainage below.

② FOX 32° 1,150'

Shorter in length and joining Wolf Gully at around 10,400', this alternative run starts from the saddle of Braddock ridge at 11,150'. Navigate sparse trees until a narrow gully develops. This run links up with Wolf at 10,400' before descending to the approach skintrack.

③ COYOTE 35° 1,050'

Below the west side of the Braddock ridgeline is a prominent, bald high point at 10,850'. Start from the north side of this knoll and sight a mix of trees and glades dropping parallel with the Fox run. This run merges with Wolf at 10,400' and continues to the drainage below.

Bearpaws Peak South

Seven Utes Mountain West
(next page)

SEVEN UTES MOUNTAIN EAST

Most of this sector is hidden from view from the highway, but quickly offers up challenging terrain when entered on the east side. Near the end of the drainage, an impressive headwall of steep chutes and tree glades awaits. This approach allows for the shortest route to summit Seven Utes Mountain via the east ridge. Seven Utes Mountain was named by a group of Arapaho who, in 1914, visited the area to record the original Indigenous names in the Cameron Pass area. Their history relates that seven Utes were killed here in an encounter with members of the Arapaho nation. *(See Oliver W. Toll's Arapaho Names and Trails, published in 1962)*

 The tight valley formed by Seven Utes and the shoulder of Braddock Peak develops both wind slabs and deep faceted snowpack layers. Careful evaluation of each aspect is necessary.

 Park at the large Seven Utes parking lot, located 4 miles west of Cameron Pass; this is inside the State Forest State Park and a state parks pass is required. This parking lot is also used by snowmobiles accessing the American Lakes area. The Colorado Mountain School maintains the Seven Utes Yurt at this location.

 Approaching the east side of Seven Utes requires careful map reading. Skin southeast out of the parking lot and immediately drop to the Michigan River. Cross a small bridge and continue south on the steepening trail. After intersecting the snowmobile road, turn left and continue steeply up the first two switchbacks. Watch for a vague trail heading due south from the snowmobile trail. Follow this vague track to the base of the Headwall Glades, approximately 1.25 miles.

 Most skiers will return via the ascent track. Snowboarders beware: you will encounter some slight uphill.

1 MAHLER GLADES 35° 500'

From any point on the west side of Mount Mahler, sight a line descending into the broad, lightly forested bowl below. The trees thicken on the lower portion and require careful route-finding.

2 HEADWALL GLADES 38° 600'

The broad headwall of the saddle between Seven Utes and Mount Mahler offers many gully and tree shots to the bowl below. The approach skintrack is usually set on this face.

3 CENTRAL GULLY 42° 900'

Central Gully is the obvious and impressive line on the east side of Seven Utes. Starting near the summit, drop straight down any of several options. Near the bottom, short cliff bands need to be negotiated.

4 SEVEN UTES CHUTES 32° 700'

After descending the north ridge of Seven Utes, scout a series of lines dropping into the creek below. There are several options, all ending along the skintrack.

5 NORTHEAST GLADES 30° 800'

From the north ridge of Seven Utes, descend a variety of treed, open slopes to the northeast. Thicker trees near the bottom are challenging. Eventually, the run intersects the approach skintrack.

Mahler Glades *(previous page)*

Headwall Area
(previous page)

SEVEN UTES MOUNTAIN WEST

ATES 3

Several proposed ski areas on this aspect attest to the steep, snowy terrain Seven Utes Mountain offers. While the ski area proposals are long gone, the north face offers a variety of steep slopes, couloirs, and tree skiing. Most of this face is visible from Hwy. 14.

The prevailing winds create large cornices on the north face of Seven Utes Mountain. Deep wind slabs often cover this aspect as well, and large avalanches have occurred. Caution is necessary.

Park at the large Seven Utes parking lot, located 4 miles west of Cameron Pass; this is inside State Forest State Park and a state parks pass is required. This lot is also used by snowmobiles accessing the American Lakes area. The Colorado Mountain School maintains the Seven Utes Yurt at this location.

Note that this approach differs slightly from the east side of Seven Utes Mountain. Skin southeast out of the parking lot and immediately drop to the Michigan River. Cross a small bridge and continue south on the steepening trail. After intersecting with the snowmobile road, continue up the snowmobile road for 1 mile. From this point, the old logging roads are vague and unmarked. Choose a switchbacking route to the northwest ridge of Seven Utes and hence to the summit.

EXIT

The most efficient return is to follow the skintrack back to the trailhead.

❶ NORTH FACE   35° 1,200'

From the summit of Seven Utes, approach the north face and select a line. The bowl eventually funnels into a steep drainage leading to the snowmobile road. Avoid the bottom of the stream bed to maintain speed.

❷ ARROW CHUTES   38° 700'

These three prominent chutes start off the northwest ridge of Seven Utes. All the options connect near the bottom. Continue downhill to the approach trail while avoiding the low-angle stream bed.

❸ NORTHWEST RIDGE   34°   800'

After ascending to the summit of Seven Utes, the skintrack down the northwest ridgeline is an ideal, low-angle return option. The upper reaches can be wind-scoured, but the lower trees and glades offer ideal options.

SEVEN UTES MOUNTAIN EAST
Image 2, Headwall

Seven Utes Summit

Headwall Glades